W9-CHL-290

Hamlet

Based on the Play by William Shakespeare
Adapted by Neil Novelli and Kathleen Forrest

SCHOLASTIC INC.

New York   Toronto   London   Auckland   Sydney
Mexico City   New Delhi   Hong Kong   Buenos Aires

**Illustrations
Tim Gabor**

Text copyright © 2003 by Scholastic Inc.
Illustrations copyright © 2003 by Tim Gabor.
All rights reserved. Published by Scholastic Inc.
Printed in the U.S.A.

ISBN 0-439-67462-X

1 0   23   13 12 11 10 09

Contents

Meet the Characters

This story takes place in Denmark. It's based on a legend that's about a thousand years old. Here are the main characters. Will any be alive by the end of the story?

Hamlet
Son of the old king and Queen Gertrude. His father's death has changed everything.

Claudius
Hamlet's uncle and the brother of the old king. He became king and married the queen.

Gertrude
Hamlet's mother and now the wife of Claudius. Could she be married to her husband's killer?

Ophelia *(oh-FEE-lia)*
Hamlet's girlfriend. But not for long. Her family wants to break them up.

Laertes *(lay-AIR-tees)*
Ophelia's older brother. He's the new king's favorite. Watch your back, Hamlet!

Polonius *(po-LO-nee-us)*
Ophelia and Laertes's father. He's the king's right-hand man.

1

A Midnight Ghost

Why can't the dead king rest in peace?

Marcellus shivered in the midnight cold. He'd been on guard outside the great stone castle since nightfall. He had a small fire, but it barely kept him warm. He was tired and afraid. He couldn't see a thing through the heavy fog.

Suddenly, his eyes grew large. He could hear something moving in the distance. "Who's there?" he shouted. "Make yourself known!"

Another guard stepped out of the fog. It was his friend, Bernardo. "Long live the king!" said Bernardo. "I'll take over now. You get some sleep."

Marcellus sighed with relief. "Never have I been so happy to see a friend!" He lowered his voice. "I was afraid that—*thing*—would appear again tonight."

"Has it?" asked Bernardo, looking serious.

Marcellus shook his head, "No." His voice rose in fear. "But what will we do if it does come? How do you fight a ghost?"

Another voice rose from the fog, laughing. "Ho! What is all this nonsense? Bernardo says you've seen a ghost. How **absurd.**" It was Horatio, a friend of young Prince Hamlet's from school.

Horatio was still laughing when, suddenly, it appeared. A ghost, dressed for battle, stepped out of the fog. The ghost looked just like Hamlet's father, the dead king of Denmark. The men could hardly breathe. Then, just as suddenly as it appeared, the ghost was gone.

Even Horatio was shaking now.

The three men huddled around the small fire and tried to figure out why the ghost had come. Lately, nothing seemed right in Denmark. Hamlet should have been crowned king after his father's death. But at the time, he had been away at school in Germany. Before Hamlet could get back home, the king's brother, Claudius, **seized** the throne. But that wasn't all. Soon after, Claudius married Hamlet's mother the queen. Hamlet's father was barely cold in his grave! Was it any surprise that the dead king was restless?

Marcellus shook his head as he shivered by the fire. "Something is rotten in the state of Denmark," he said.

Suddenly, the ghost appeared again! Horatio wanted to run. But he fought back his fear and found the courage to speak.

"T-t-tell me," Horatio cried out. "Why have you come to us?"

But the ghost just stared with blank eyes before disappearing into the night.

"I must go to Hamlet," Horatio told the others. "If the ghost will not speak to me, surely, he will speak to his own son."

Heads Up!

Think about what Claudius has done. Then make a prediction about what the ghost might say to Hamlet.

Suddenly, the ghost appears again!

2

The New King Rules

Hamlet's worst enemy is now the man in charge.

King Claudius ordered that the castle's great hall be brightly lit with blazing torches. His family and advisers were laughing and talking while they waited for one last guest to arrive. The members of the royal court had been called for an announcement.

Finally, Prince Hamlet walked in the door, and the laughter hushed. Hamlet was dressed in black and his face looked grim. He wore black clothes in honor of his father's death. Everyone looked away, except for Ophelia. She was the beautiful daughter of the new king's adviser, Polonius. Hamlet loved Ophelia. She was, he thought, the only one in the room who could understand his **misery.**

King Claudius began speaking in a powerful voice. "You know I loved my brother," he announced. "And I know you loved your king. We could **mourn** his death forever, but we must do what's best for the kingdom and move on. That is why I have taken Queen Gertrude as my wife. I know we have your best wishes, and I thank you for that."

Hamlet **scowled.** My father had loved my mother deeply, he thought. It isn't right that she should marry so soon after his death.

King Claudius deepened his voice. "I thought you all should know that the kingdom is in danger. Young Fortinbras of Norway plans to attack. He thinks we can be defeated easily now that the old king is dead. But he has not yet met the new king!"

Hamlet saw his mother, the queen, smile proudly at her new husband. "He's half the man my father was," Hamlet muttered to himself. "How can she look at him that way?"

While Hamlet was thinking these dark thoughts, everyone else was cheering. Claudius **beamed** and glanced across the room at Polonius, his trusted adviser. Ophelia and her older brother, Laertes, stood with him.

Claudius smiled and called out, "Come here, Laertes. I understand you want to ask me for a favor. Don't be shy. Ask and it shall be yours."

Laertes kneeled before the king, "Your Majesty, I ask your permission to leave Denmark and return to school in France."

King Claudius smiled and said, "Yes, of course! This is the best time of your life. Go back to school and enjoy yourself."

Hamlet could barely hide his anger. Claudius had insisted that he remain at the castle. Now he was letting Laertes return to school. Hamlet **fumed** in silence, feeling like a prisoner in his own home. But what could Hamlet say? His uncle was now king.

Claudius turned to Hamlet. "Now, Hamlet," he boomed. "Why so gloomy?"

Then the Queen added in a soft voice: "Dear son, you've worn those black clothes long enough. We have already suffered so much sadness. Why do you seem to be taking your father's death so badly?"

Laertes kneels before the king.

"*Seem*, Mother?" Hamlet spoke sharply. "This is not an act! Anyone can cry and *pretend* to be sad, but the pain I have inside is real. This is not pretending."

Claudius stepped in. "Hamlet, mourning will not bring the dead back to life. You must move on and accept me as your father. If you do, I'll love you like a son."

King Claudius smiled again and put his arm around the young prince's shoulders. Hamlet twisted away in **disgust,** but said nothing.

"Our dear son Hamlet has agreed to remain here in Denmark," the king announced. "Now let's all celebrate!"

Heads Up!

King Claudius smiles a lot. Is he as nice as he wants people to think? What does Hamlet think?

3

Forbidden Love

Will Ophelia dump Hamlet?

Laertes was all packed to leave for school and excited to go, but he was worried about Ophelia. His younger sister loved Hamlet, and Hamlet said he loved her. But Laertes knew how quickly a young man could change his mind. Hamlet might walk away and leave Ophelia with a broken heart.

Laertes hugged his sister. "You must remember something while I'm gone," he said.

"What is so important?" Ophelia teased.

"I'm serious," said Laertes. "I don't think you can trust Hamlet. He says he loves you now, and perhaps he does. But men are **fickle** and I don't want my little sister to be hurt."

Ophelia smiled. "I will keep that in mind, big brother. But if you keep talking, your boat will leave without you."

At that moment, their father, Polonius, burst into the room. Laertes wished he had left sooner. He was hoping to be spared his father's words of advice, which he had heard many times before.

"Son, hurry and get on board your ship," Polonius said. "But first, I want you to remember a few things." Laertes rolled his eyes.

"Dress well and be **loyal** to your friends," his father said. "Don't borrow money or lend money. Don't get into fights, but if you do, fight bravely. And above all, be true to yourself. Now, stop waiting around and go catch your ship!"

Laertes smiled and hugged his father, then picked up his suitcase.

"Good-bye, Ophelia," Laertes called out. Then softly he added, "Remember what I told you."

Father's Orders

"What did Laertes say to you?" Polonius asked after his son had gone.

Ophelia didn't want to say. She wanted to keep her feelings for Hamlet private.

"Oh, it was just something about Hamlet," said Ophelia **vaguely.**

"Hamlet!" growled Polonius. "I've been meaning to talk to you about him! Young men have only one thing in mind, and they'll promise anything to get it."

"But father," she said. "We love each other, and he has even talked about marriage."

"Marriage!" Polonius exploded. "Don't be such a foolish girl! Hamlet is a prince. He must marry royalty. He cannot choose his own wife."

Polonius added coldly, "You must break it off with Hamlet. Do not write to him, or answer his letters, or keep his gifts. That is final!"

Ophelia could barely breathe. Her father was ruining her whole life.

"I will obey you, father," was all she could say as she ran from the room.

Heads Up!

Hamlet said Ophelia is the only one who understands his misery. How do you think he'll react to not being able to see her?

4

The Ghost Speaks

The ghost has a secret—and a job for Hamlet.

Out on the castle wall, Hamlet stood with Horatio and the two soldiers, Marcellus and Bernardo. It was midnight and freezing cold.

"Did the ghost truly look like my father?" Hamlet asked.

"Yes, sir," Bernardo said.

Just as Hamlet opened his mouth to respond, the ghost rose out of the dark, shimmering in the torch light. The ghost looked straight at Hamlet and signaled to him. Then it turned and began to float away.

The soldiers tried to hold Hamlet back, but he broke loose and ran after the ghost.

Hamlet followed it deep into the night, out of sight of the others. Finally, it stopped and turned. To Hamlet, it seemed as if his father were alive

To Hamlet, it seems as if his father is alive again.

again and looking him right in the eye.

"Father," Hamlet gasped in shock, "why have you come back?"

"There is something you must do for me, son," the ghost said. "Your uncle, Claudius, is a liar and a murderer."

"A murderer!" Hamlet cried. "Father, what do you mean?"

"The day I died, I was resting in my garden," said the ghost. "While I slept, Claudius crept up and poured a deadly poison in my ear. It appeared that I had been bitten by a snake. But the snake, in fact, was Claudius."

Hamlet was stunned. "What must I do?"

"Take **revenge,**" the ghost ordered. "Kill your uncle. But let your mother rest." Then the ghost began to fade. "And remember me, always," it called. Then it **vanished.**

"Remember you!" Hamlet said and bent his head, "of course I will, father—always!"

A few moments later, Horatio, Bernardo, and Marcellus caught up with Hamlet.

"Are you all right?" Horatio gasped.

Hamlet was tearing at his hair. His eyes had a wild look that his friends had never seen.

"You must promise me one thing," Hamlet growled at them. "Never tell anyone what happened here tonight. Never!"

The men stepped back out of fear. Hamlet seemed suddenly changed. They looked at each other not knowing what to say.

"Promise!" screamed Hamlet.

"Never, Prince Hamlet," the men said finally. "Never a word of it."

Heads Up!

Why does Hamlet want to keep the ghost a secret? What do you think Claudius would do if he found out what Hamlet knew?

CHAPTER

5

· ·

Playing the Fool

Is Hamlet losing it? Or is it all an act?

After the ghost's visit, Hamlet could barely sleep and often forgot to eat. Here he was, locked in his own home with the man who killed his father. And worse, his own mother had married the murderer. He must get revenge for his dead father's sake.

But should he really kill his uncle? What if the ghost had been lying? What if he imagined the whole thing? How could he know for sure?

Hamlet needed time to think, but he worried that Claudius would get **suspicious.** Wandering the halls at night, he came up with a plan. "If I play the fool," he said to himself, "people will laugh and pity me. No one will guess what's on my mind. Besides, it's not really a lie. I am half-crazy with **indecision.**"

For days, Hamlet stumbled around in wrinkled clothes. He didn't wash or comb his hair. People began to laugh and whisper.

But Claudius kept a close watch on Hamlet. The prince, after all, had a right to the throne. Suppose he was up to something?

Love Sick?

Ever since he had met the ghost, Hamlet had been trying to speak to Ophelia about it, but she had been avoiding him. Finally he caught up with her. He took her face gently between his hands. His eyes searched hers, and he saw tears.

"How can I drag her into this?" he thought. "If I tell her about my father's murder, then she will be in danger, too."

He shook his head sadly and backed away.

When he was nearly out of sight, Ophelia heard a horrifying sound. A cry of **anguish** rang

---

─Heads Up!─
Hamlet decides to play the fool to buy some time. But does it seem as if he is losing control? Explain.

out against the castle walls. She felt a chill run through her. What they were saying must be true. Hamlet had snapped. She ran to tell her father what had happened.

"That's it," thought Polonius. "That's what has been wrong with Prince Hamlet."

Polonius went straight to the king. Naturally, Claudius was worried about his nephew's strange behavior. But Polonius thought that the king was worried about Hamlet's health.

"Your Majesty," he said feeling pleased with himself. "I know what troubles Hamlet. The prince is sick with love. My daughter Ophelia has refused him, and it is driving him mad."

"How can we be sure?" Claudius asked.

Polonius thought for a moment. "I could send my daughter to talk to Hamlet," he said. "You and I shall hide behind a curtain and listen. That will reveal all."

Heads Up!

Polonius thinks Claudius is worried about Hamlet's health. What is the king really worried about?

CHAPTER

6

Behind the Curtain

Hamlet has a special message for Claudius.

Hamlet sat in his room staring blankly at a book, but he couldn't concentrate. He couldn't eat or sleep. All night, he lay awake wondering what to do. His mother seemed like a stranger, and Ophelia never even looked at him now. Oh, why did his father have to die?

He stood up and began to pace, tugging at his hair as he walked. "To be, or not to be," he wondered out loud. "That is the question. Would it be braver to suffer through all these troubles? Or should I end my sorrows in death and sink into a long, peaceful sleep."

He stopped pacing. "But what about dreams? That's the tricky part. What if I end up stuck inside a nightmare that goes on forever?

No. It's better to face the problems I have

now than end up suffering new troubles that are even worse." He stared at a painting of his father on the wall, "I will decide. Then I will act."

The sound of footsteps startled him. He turned to see Ophelia standing there. She was as beautiful as ever. Did she finally wish to talk to him? Did that mean she still loved him?

She bowed and said, "My Lord." Without even looking at him, she held out a package.

"Here are the gifts you've given me," she said. "I don't wish to have them any more." She seemed unhappy and spoke stiffly. It was as if she were being forced to say these words.

Ophelia went on speaking, sounding as though she were reading lines from a play. But Hamlet wasn't listening. He was already suspicious of Claudius and Polonius. Could they be using Ophelia to get to him? Was this all a trick?

Hamlet pulled back his hand and let the package drop. "I never gave you any gifts," he said, speaking coldly.

"My Lord," she said, "you know you did. You said you loved me." Now she seemed confused.

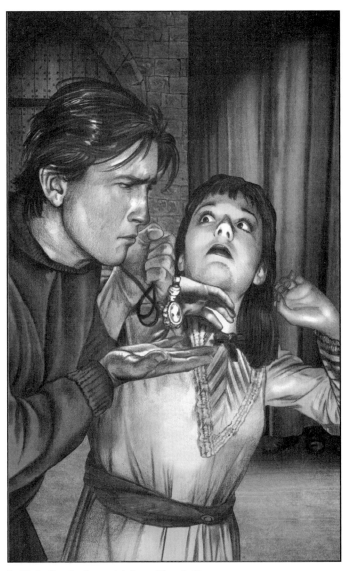

Is Ophelia playing a trick on Hamlet?

"I loved you?" he said. "You? No, never."
It hurt him to talk to her this way. But he was
sure that she had **betrayed** him.

Ophelia said nothing and looked at the floor.

"You know, you'd be better off if you ran away
and became a nun," said Hamlet. "Men are all
liars. You should stay away from us all." Then he
asked, "Where is your father?"

Ophelia swallowed hard and looked around.
She stuttered, "M-my father is at home, my lord."

"Well," said Hamlet, "let the old fool stay
home where he's safe!"

Hamlet stormed out, and Ophelia ran from the
room, sobbing.

Polonius and Claudius stepped out from
behind a curtain.

"See, Your Majesty," Polonius said, "love has
driven him mad."

Heads Up!

*Hamlet says that Polonius had better stay
home where he's safe. How do you think
Claudius felt when he heard that?*

Claudius nodded, but he didn't believe that for one minute. "No," he thought, "Hamlet isn't crazy. The prince is troubled, but what's on his mind has nothing to do with love. The boy is definitely a danger to me."

That left only one thing to do. Claudius would have to get rid of Hamlet first.

7

A Trap for the King

Claudius starts to sweat.

The next morning, a group of traveling actors came through the castle gate, juggling, playing music, and dancing.

"Come and watch the greatest show on earth!" said the leader. "We can make you laugh and cry."

Hamlet heard the noise and came out. The actors often performed at his school, so he knew them well.

Suddenly, Hamlet knew what he would do.

"Can you put on a play at the castle tonight?" he asked the lead actor.

"It would be our pleasure, my lord."

"I'd like to write a scene for you," said Hamlet. "It's about something that has special meaning for me. Can you learn it fast?"

"Of course, my lord," the actor said.

That night, everyone at the castle gathered to see the play. For the first time in weeks, Hamlet was smiling.

Two actors appeared on stage, one dressed as a king, the other as a queen.

"Ah," said the king. "We have been married for many years, my love. But now I am sick, and soon you will marry another man."

"No, never!" said the queen. "I would rather die than marry again."

The actors continued with their dramatic speeches of love. Hamlet sat in silence, watching Claudius in the dim light. Claudius was the only one not smiling.

"I am tired now," announced the king in the play. He went to sleep on a bench, and the queen left the stage.

Now a third actor walked onto the stage. He carried a small bottle in his hand.

─**Heads Up!**─

Hamlet wants to learn the truth. How will this play help him figure it out?

"Aha!" he said. "Now is my chance!" He gave an evil laugh. "This poison will kill the king, and no one will ever know."

Slowly, the actor pretended to empty the bottle into the sleeping king's ear. Suddenly, Claudius stood up in the darkness, shaking. Hamlet had been watching him the whole time.

"Stop this nonsense now!" Claudius shouted. Then he ran like a man afraid for his life.

Gertrude and the rest of the court followed after him. Only Hamlet and Horatio stayed behind. The prince turned to his friend, and for the first time in weeks, he laughed. But it wasn't exactly a happy laugh. Hamlet had forced Claudius to watch his crime acted out on stage. And Claudius had cracked.

Heads Up!

Hamlet thinks he has proven that Claudius killed his father. Why does that make him feel so much better?

Claudius runs like a man afraid for his life.

8

The First Strike

Hamlet takes action.

Later that night, Queen Gertrude was in **despair.** She knew Hamlet had done something to upset her new husband, though she didn't know what...or why they couldn't get along.

"What is wrong with Hamlet?" she asked Polonius. "Please tell me what I can do."

Polonius still believed Hamlet was suffering from a broken heart. "Send for Prince Hamlet," he said. "Talk to him and you will see."

Once again, Polonius hid behind a curtain.

Hamlet arrived, looking ready for a fight. "What is it, mother?" he asked.

"Hamlet, why must you treat your uncle this way?" she demanded. "Claudius is a good man."

"A good man!" yelled Hamlet. "Hah! How can you be so blind?"

Hamlet pushed his mother into a chair and shoved his face close to hers. "Listen to me, please!" He was screaming and begging.

Gertrude was shocked. "Help!" she screamed.

Polonius heard her from behind the curtain. He got so scared that he forgot he was supposed to be hiding. He began to call for help, too.

Hamlet heard a voice and thought it was Claudius. Hamlet drew his sword and ran it through the curtain.

The curtains parted and Polonius slumped to the ground, dying. Hamlet looked down at the king's advisor coldly.

"You should have been more careful choosing your friends," he said to Polonius.

Gertrude began to sob.

"You *should* cry," said Hamlet. He turned and pointed to a painting of the old king. "That," he said, "is my father. He was a brave and honest man. Now he is dead and you are married to the man who murdered him!"

"Please, Hamlet," the queen begged, "do not say such things. You're breaking my heart!"

"Believe me, mother." Hamlet pleaded.

Hamlet looks down at the king's advisor coldly.

"If this is so," the queen said in a shaky voice, "then you have to tell me what to do." She looked lost and confused.

"Beware of your new husband," Hamlet said. "And if my words have convinced you, then do not tell him what I know."

Hamlet stormed out, leaving his mother slumped in her chair.

Heads Up!

Hamlet finally confronts his mother directly. Do you think she believes him?

9

An Evil Plot

Claudius has a plan. Will Hamlet survive it?

Hamlet woke with a start on a boat in the middle of the sea. It had been three days since he had killed Polonius. He knew the king had wanted to put him in jail—or worse. But Hamlet was loved by the queen and the people, so Claudius sent him to England instead.

Sleeping next to Hamlet were two friends from school, Rosencrantz and Guildenstern. The king had sent them along to keep Hamlet company. But the prince knew better. Since Claudius had sent them, Hamlet didn't trust them.

Hamlet rose quietly and opened the bag that Guildenstern had with him. In it, was a letter from Claudius to the king of England.

It said simply, "As a favor to Denmark, kill Prince Hamlet."

Hamlet carefully rewrote the letter to say, "As a favor to Denmark, kill Rosencrantz and Guildenstern!" Then he put the letter back.

Back to Denmark

The next day, Hamlet awoke to the sound of cannon fire. Pirates were attacking!

Hamlet drew his sword and leaped over the railing onto the pirates' ship. But then wind drove the two ships apart. Hamlet was stranded alone with the pirates!

Hamlet stood facing them. Then he began to laugh. "I have no **quarrel** with you gentlemen," he said. "I know who my real enemies are." Then Hamlet added, "Would someone mind loaning me some clothes? I'm tired of wearing black. And later, when you return me to Denmark, I will pay you well."

—Heads Up!—
What problems does Claudius hope to solve by sending Hamlet to England?

10

Laertes Seeks Revenge

Hamlet better watch his back.

While Hamlet was gone, poor Ophelia spent days walking alone through the woods and fields. She had lost her only love, and now she had lost her father, too.

Bit by bit, Ophelia's sad eyes stopped seeing the world. She saw only the pain inside her. She rarely stopped weeping.

One day, she saw some flowers by the river. As she bent down to pick them, she felt herself falling into the water. She let herself go limp. Quickly, the current swept her under, away from all the troubles of Denmark.

Later that day, Laertes returned from school and went to see the king. He was furious about his father's death and swore he would have his revenge on Hamlet.

Quickly the current sweeps Ophelia under.

"I am sorry for you, Laertes," said the king. "But there is worse news. Your sister is dead. She was not herself after your father's death. People say she did not wish to live anymore."

Laertes cried out and started to run for the door, but Claudius blocked his way. "Wait, I have a plan," the king whispered. "But you have to listen to me."

"Tell me what I must do," Laertes said.

This is just the moment that Claudius had been waiting for. He had gotten word that his plot against Hamlet had failed. But Laertes would now help him succeed at last.

"You and Hamlet shall have a friendly sword match," Claudius told him.

"Friendly!" yelled Laertes.

"Listen to me!" Claudius ordered. "Hamlet's sword will be dull. Yours will be sharp and we shall poison the tip. Give Hamlet a small scratch, and he will die! In case that fails, I'll poison his drink as well. Either way, Hamlet does not have long to live."

"Alright, then!" said Laertes. "I'll challenge Hamlet to a *friendly* match."

Heads Up!

Claudius is using Laertes to get at Hamlet. But why?

11

Graveyard Battle

Laertes and Hamlet's grudge match.

Hamlet arrived back in Denmark and immediately found Horatio. The two men went for a walk, and Hamlet told his friend all that had happened with the letter and with the pirates. Horatio wanted to tell Hamlet about Ophelia, but he couldn't find the words.

As they passed through the castle graveyard, Hamlet saw a man digging a new grave.

"Whose grave is that?" Hamlet asked.

"My grave," the worker joked.

Hamlet teased back. "It can't be your grave," he said, "You're still alive."

"Well, I'm the one who's making it," said the worker. "So it's mine." And he shoveled more dirt.

Hamlet wondered whose grave it really was. Then he saw six men carrying a coffin. The king, the queen, and Laertes followed. Behind them was the entire court. Hamlet searched for Ophelia but couldn't find her anywhere. Hamlet looked at Horatio. His friend nodded sadly. That's when Hamlet realized that this was her funeral.

Suddenly, Laertes leaped into the grave after the coffin. He was weeping, half crazy with grief.

"Who cries out in such grief!" Hamlet cried, jumping in after Laertes. "No one feels this sorrow more than I!"

The two began to fight while the mourners looked on in horror.

"Hamlet!" screamed Gertrude.

"Stop this!" Claudius yelled. "Guards! Pull them apart!"

"I loved her more than forty thousand brothers could," said Hamlet as he let Horatio lead him away.

"Be patient," Claudius whispered to Laertes. "You will get your turn."

The mourners look on in horror.

12

Bloodbath at the Castle

Revenge is not sweet.

A week after the funeral, the mood at the castle was much brighter. A feast was set out on a huge table in the great hall. Trumpets sounded as the king and queen entered. Hamlet and Laertes' friendly sword match was about to begin.

Laertes looked nervous. His eyes darted around the room.

"I'm sorry about your sister," Hamlet said to Laertes. He felt no anger toward him. But he had a bad feeling about the match.

The match began and the men leaped and dodged. Time after time, Hamlet touched Laertes with the tip of his sword. But Laertes couldn't get near Hamlet. Finally, the men took a break.

"Why don't you have a drink?" asked the king. He motioned to the poisoned cup.

"Not just yet," said Hamlet.

"I'll have it," said Gertrude taking the cup.

"Gertrude, no!" yelled Claudius, as the queen raised it to her lips. But it was too late.

Just then, Laertes leaped at Hamlet from behind. He only managed to scratch Hamlet slightly on the wrist. But this made Hamlet furious. Hamlet grabbed the sword from Laertes and slashed his opponent's arm with it. Then Hamlet spun around.

"Hamlet! I'm dying! That drink was poisoned!" Gertrude coughed out.

Then Laertes sank to the floor. "Hamlet," he said. "My sword was poisoned. You will die from that cut, too. Claudius is to blame. Please forgive me," he whispered. Then he died.

Claudius moved to Hamlet's side. "Hamlet," he said, "there is no truth in that."

The king smiled and drew a hidden **dagger.** But before he could use it, Hamlet rose up and finished him with the poisoned sword.

"Help my friends, I am hurt!" cried Claudius. He tried to crawl to Gertrude, but he fell flat, gasping for air. Then his breathing stopped.

Hamlet could feel the poison working on him, too. He called Horatio to his side.

"My friend," he said breathing hard, "make sure the world hears my story. They must know the truth."

At that moment, trumpets sounded. The doors opened, and Fortinbras of Norway entered with his soldiers.

"Fortinbras shall have the kingdom of Denmark," Hamlet whispered. Then he died.

The room was silent. Fortinbras walked over to Hamlet. He knelt by the body.

"Hamlet was a **noble** prince," said Fortinbras. "We will bury him with royal honors."

"And now," he said, turning to Horatio, "tell me what happened to our friend, Hamlet."

Heads Up!

Look up noble *in the glossary. Why do you think Fortinbras calls Hamlet noble?*

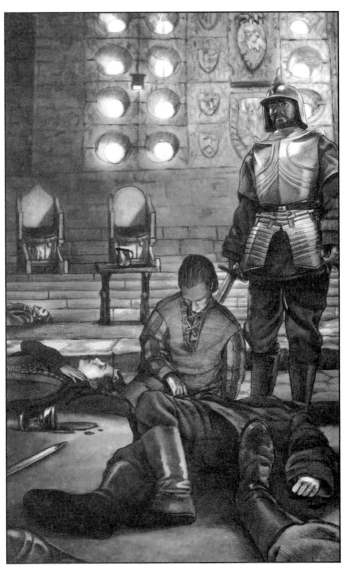

The room is as silent as death.

William Shakespeare

(1564–1616)

William Shakespeare is considered the finest writer in the English language. About 400 years ago, his plays were as popular as big, blockbuster movies are today. He wrote about wise fools and evil kings. He wrote about unlucky lovers and happy couples. All kinds of people—rich and poor—wanted to see his plays. His plays were so popular that they were even performed for the king, just like the play in *Hamlet*.

Shakespeare wrote plays with happy endings called comedies. He also wrote plays like *Hamlet,* which are called **tragedies.** A tragedy is a story about suffering and loss. The heroes fight bravely against a situation that they cannot control. They make mistakes but they are basically good people. The story is sad, but the audience was meant to learn from it. Other famous tragedies by Shakespeare include *Romeo and Juliet, Macbeth*, and *Othello*.

Glossary

absurd *(adjective)* silly, not making sense

anguish *(noun)* a strong feeling of pain

beam *(verb)* to smile brightly

betray *(verb)* to hurt someone who had trusted you

dagger *(noun)* a small, sharp knife

despair *(noun)* a feeling of great sadness without having any hope

disgust *(noun)* a strong feeling of dislike

fickle *(adjective)* not faithful or true

fume *(verb)* to burn with anger

indecision *(noun)* not being able to decide

loyal *(adjective)* faithful or true

misery *(noun)* a deep sadness

mourn *(verb)* to show sadness over someone's death

noble *(adjective)* from a royal or high-ranking family; acting in an idealistic or high-minded way

Glossary

quarrel *(noun)* an argument

revenge *(noun)* getting back at someone who did something to hurt you

seize *(verb)* to take by force

scowl *(verb)* to frown in an angry way

suspicious *(adjective)* thinking that something is not the way it seems

tragedy *(noun)* a play or situation that has an unhappy ending that couldn't be avoided

vaguely *(adverb)* in a way that is not clear or exact

vanish *(verb)* to disappear